GW01316160

Table of Contents

INTRODUCTION

History of American football

The game we know today as American football came into being, borne out of the English sports of soccer and rugby. What was created in the late 19th century is now incredibly popular with millions watching games, betting on games, and scrambling the internet to find the NFL playoff odds. It is incredible to think of how quickly this game grew so much. When, only in the late 19th century were elite Northeastern colleges taking up the sport, playing a soccer-styled game with rules adopted from the London Football Association. Intercollegiate matches began to spring up in schools such as Rutgers, Princeton, Harvard and so on. Rugby-type rules ended up becoming more preferential among school and spectators alike, and from here the game grew.

The father of American football

A man named Walter Camp is considered to be the most important person in the development of American football. As a youth he excelled in many sports. Following the introduction of rugby styled rules to American Football, he became a fixture at the Massasoit House conventions, where rules were debated and changed. Dissatisfied with what seemed to him to basically be a disorganized mob, he proposed his first change at the first meeting he ever attended in 1878: which was a reduction in the number of players from 15 to 11. However, the motion was initially rejected at that time, however it passed three years later. The effect was in idea to open up the game and emphasize speed over strength. His most famous change however was the establishing of the line of scrimmage and the snap from center to quarterback, which is still one of the coolest parts of the game to this day. This motion was also carried in 1880. He changed the rules of football, and innovated the game into what we recognize as football today. Though this was long ago and many things have still changed since, he revolutionized the sport and brought much change that made it less like soccer and rugby, and its own, unique sport which we all know and love.

Growth of professional football

Professional football started to grow even more in the early 20th century, as the general population in the U.S. started to slowly fall in love with the sport. It became the subject of intense competition and rivalries. Then in 1920 we saw the American Professional Football Association founded, in a meeting at a Hupmobile car dealership in Canton, Ohio. Jim Thorpe was elected as the league's first president and after several more meetings the league's membership was formalized. In the early years of the league, it was little more than a formal agreement between the teams to play one another and declare a champion at the season's end. And teams were still permitted to play non-league members. The league expanded quickly. In 1921 several more teams joined, increasing the membership to 22 teams altogether, among these were the Green Bay Packers, which is the team with the record for the longest use of an unchanged name. While the NFL was founded in 1920 the AFL was founded in 1959, and so began a rivalry that ended in 1970.

The Merger (1970)

That brings us to 1970, the merge that ended the issues between the AFL and NFL. The two leagues decided to merge in 1970, leading to the creation of the NFL we know today. The AFL and NFL changed their names to the NFC (National Football Conference) and the AFC changed their name to the AFC (American Football Conference). The NFL continued to grow, adopting some innovations of the AFL, including the two-point conversion. It also expanded several times to reach its current 32-team membership, with 16 teams in each conference. Each of these two conferences has four divisions, north, east, south, and west, and each division homes four teams. Since the NFL merger that created the sport we know and love today, it has grown incredibly. The Super Bowl has become a cultural phenomenon across the country, and even across the world, and it is also one of the most popular events televised in the United States. It is also a major source of advertising as well. The NFL has grown from a tiny idea, contributed to by many, and fathered by people with a dream in the 19th century, to an incredibly popular spectator sport. However, it is safe to say that it is doubtful that the sport would have reached the incredible heights it has today without the intervention of the 1970 merger that brought the NFL and AFL together to create the countrywide NFL that brings the whole country together in an unforgettable season of sport.

Football we know today

The sport we know and love today was born a very long time ago, and some may even say that cultures before the America we know today, played similar sports, however, what we know as American football, and the rules and way it is played, was carefully formulated by many masterminds. The sport was influenced by many, which can be seen in the game today, rules chosen and crafted by the father of football Walter Camp. The merger of the AFL and NFL in 1970, which changed the rivalry and made the sport even bigger. Vince Lombardi – the coach of the Green Bay Packers, who won the first two Super Bowls and ended up having the trophy named after him in his passing. The rise of this sport took less than two centuries in the making, and now it is the biggest sport in the U.S. In fact, it is estimated that in 2021 the franchise of the NFL is almost priceless. The most valuable teams have net worth in the billions, such as the Dallas Cowboys at $6.5 billion, and the New England Patriots at $5 billion. No matter how it began, and how long it took, we know you will be bouncing for this season's Super Bowl, and so will we. As we thank everyone involved in the creation of this incredible sport.

Primarily, to have an American football match, the basic equipment required is the American football called the Ovoid ball.

Ovoid ball − the ball used for the play is an egg-shaped brown colored ball called the Ovoid ball. It is 11 inches or 35 centimeters in length from tip to tip and 22 inches or 55 centimeters in circumference at the center of the ball. The ball weighs about 450gms and inflated to a pressure of 0.6 to 1.1 atmospheres. Apart from the ball the players need to put on some protective equipment to compete in the game.

• Helmet − Comprises of jaw pads, an integrated face mask, chin strap, mouth guard and particular shock absorbents to reduce the force of impacts of the ball.

• Shoulder Pads − A key equipment with hard outer made of plastic and shock absorbing foam inside, gives the players a broad-shouldered look.

• Arm Pads − Light and flexible arm pads help the players to be bruise free

• Elbow Pads − Protect and deforms the impact with its skin-tight webbing.

• Rib pads − Absorb and distribute the shock through the rib pad specially designed to normalize players body temperatures and protects against injuries.

• Hip & tailbone pads − Are put into the pouches of the belt worn under the pants.

• Thigh & knee Pads − Quilted pads made of plastic and foam and are put into the pockets stitched inside the pants

• Gloves − Hand gloves are not mandatory for the players but the thick padding linen helps to protect fingers and hands.

• Cleats (footgear) − Players need perfect sole footwear with spikes called "cleats" below the sole designed specifically for games on the grass.

• Jersey − A nylon material loose colored shirt with colored side panels are worn by all the players. Usually the players name and number are mentioned by his team color.

• Pants − A nylon mesh colored pant with four individual pockets on the inner side of the pant to hold thigh & knee pads. Hip and tailbone pads with a safety belt to secure the pads is also provided.

American Football - Terms

Before knowing the game rules and playing guidelines, it's very important to get familiarized with the terms used in the game.

• Tee – a cone shaped platform which holds the ball

• Yard Space – Space gained by the player to measure the progress of the game.

• Line of Scrimmage – The lines parallel to goal line and next to each team's end, the two lines are termed as the offensive & defensive line of scrimmage.

• Offense – Team with the control of the ball.

• Defense – Team opposing the offense, without the possession of the ball.

• Center – Player in the offense, with the control of the ball

• Tackle player – Position of the players on both offense and defence lines.

• Tight end – Position of offensive team player also called as the Y receiver, placed next to the offensive tackle.

• Wide Receiver – Position of offensive team player 7 yards away from the formation.

• Quarterback – Position of offensive player right behind the centre.

• Halfback – Position of offensive player behind the wide receiver near to the goal line.

• Fullback – Position of offensive player placed behind the quarterback in forming a T shape structure.

• End player – Position of defensive player placed on the defensive line of scrimmage exactly opposing the centre.

• Nose tackle – Position of the defensive player opposing the centre, effective in stopping the running and rushing the pass.

• Linebacker – Position of defensive player placed right behind the end players.

• Cornerback – Position of defensive player positioned behind the linebackers to disrupt the passing.

• Safeties – Position of defensive player behind the linebacker ready to take control of the ball from the offense.

• Dead ball – The ball not anymore in the play

• Kickoff – The ball is placed on a tee at the defense's 35-yard line, and a special kicker also kicks the ball to the offense.

• Placekick – It is a style of kicking the ball when put on the tee.

• Drop kick – When the ball is being dropped to the ground and is being kicked before it hits the ground again.

• Free kick – It is a kicking form to place the ball in the play.

• Down − Time period in which the individual plays in a certain duration, outside of which the ball is dead or not in play.

• First Down − When the offensive team effectively passes and moves the ball 10 or more yards, they earn a first down.

• Run − A player advancing the ball gaining the necessary yard space.

• Pass − A player passes the control of the ball to other player of the same team.

• Forward pass − A player passing the ball, might touch an object, a person, or the ground nearer to the other team's end line or is unintentionally lost in a forward throwing motion.

• Tackle − When the player holding the ball whose knee touches the ground the play comes to an end with tackle.

• Touchdown − It is a scoring system worth 6 points ideally when a player carries the ball and touches the opponent's end zone

• Point after touchdown (PAT) − After the touchdown the team will try for an extra 1 or 2 points by kicking the ball through the goal post or throwing it to the end zone.

• Field Goal − Worth of 3 points occurs if the ball is place kicked, drop kicked or free kicked in between the goal posts in the opponent's end zone.

• Safety − Scoring system worth of 2 points occurs by making the player possessing the ball out of his own end zone and out of bounds, or driving the other team to fumble the ball to exit the end zone. A safety is also presented if the offensive team does a foul in its own end zone.

• Turnover − Happens when one team loses the ball the other team gains.

• Fumble − Occurs when the player drops the ball by chance.

• Interception − Takes place when a player regains the ownership of the ball from an opposing player.

Rules of American Football

• Games last for four 15 minute quarters. A 2 minute break between the 1st & 2nd and 3rd & 4th quarters is had along with a 15 minute rest between 2nd and 3rd quarters (half time).

• Each team has 4 downs to gain 10 or more yards. They can either throw or run the ball to make the yards. As soon as the team gains the required yards then the downs reset and the yardage resets. Failure to make the yardage after 4 downs will result in a turnover.

• There are hundreds of different plays that players can run on any down. Plays are made up by the teams and often have players running all over the place (routes) in what is essentially organised chaos. The head coach or quarter back calls the on field plays for the attacking team whilst the defensive captain calls the plays for the defensive team.

• At the start of every game is the coin toss to decide which team receives the ball first and which side of the pitch they want to start from.

• The game begins with a kick-off where one team punts the ball down field for the other team to then run back with the ball as far as possible.

• On fourth down the offence has the option to either try to make up the yards they are short or to kick the ball. If they decide to kick they have two options; to punt or to try for a field goal. Depending on their position on the pitch will usually dictate their paly. Anything within 40 yards or so of the opposition's goal posts will result in a field goal attempt. Further back will likely mean they take the punt option.

Basic American Football Rules

To a newcomer, American football can look overly complex. However, the fundamentals of the game are very easy to understand and follow. Here is our guide to the basic rules of the game, including the flow of play and the methods of scoring. It should equip you with enough information to enable you to enjoy watching or even playing American football, while you learn the more in depth nuances of the game.

The game

Normal play consists of two teams of 11 players on field (one on offence the other on defense) competing during four 15 minute quarters. There are usually three 'time-outs' per half for each team, with a 12 minutes half-time interval. The purpose of the game is to move the ball into the opposition's 'end zone', either by running with the ball until tackled, or by passing the ball to a teammate downfield, towards the end zone. Although there are only 11 players from each side on the field at any one time, a team is actually made up of 45 players. The key player on each side is the quarterback who attempts to dictate play.

Downs

Downs are the part of the game which often needlessly confuses newcomers. They are actually fairly straightforward. In a nutshell, the rule is as follows:

• The team in possession of the ball (offence) needs to move the ball forward by at least 10 yards while they are on offence. This is why the pitch has clearly marked yardage lines on it.

• They have four chances, or downs, to gain those 10 yards and if they advance the ball that far, the count resets and the team earns another set of four downs to try go a further 10 yards.

• If the offensive team fails to move these 10 yards within four downs, possession is then given up and the defensive side gets their turn to play offense. Teams will usually kick for a field goal or downfield to the defending team on the fourth down to try and salvage some points before they lose possession.

Scoring in American football

The ultimate aim in American football is similar to pretty much every other sport out there – to score more points than the opposition. Scoring is worked out in the game as follows:

Touchdown (6 Points)

• A touchdown is scored when a team crosses the opposition's goal line with the ball, or catches or collects the ball in the end zone.

Field Goal (3 Points)

• A team will usually attempt these on the fourth down - if the kicker is close enough to the end zone to kick the ball through between the upright posts.

Extra Point (1 Or 2 Points)

• An extra point is earned by kicking the ball through the uprights after a touchdown (it's similar to a conversion in rugby). Two points are earned by taking the ball into the end zone again, but since it is more difficult, most teams opt to take the 1pt.

Safety (2 Points)

• The defensive team can gain 2 pts if they tackle a member of the offensive team with the ball in their own end zone.

I hope this guide has armed you with the necessary tools to get to grips with the game. As with any other sport, football has numerous other elements and rules in addition to the ones outlined here, but by understanding the flow of the game and the scoring, you should be able to at least enjoy and understand it as you fill in the gaps.

Duration

College and pro football games last 60 minutes, and the game is divided into 4 quarters of 15 minutes each. High school games last 48 minutes and are divided into 12-minute quarters. The clock runs unless the officials signal it must be stopped for incomplete passes or plays that go out of bounds. The officials also stop the clock when they need to measure the placement of the ball to see if the offense advanced it 10 yards.

Each team gets 3 time-outs per half.

If the game is tied at the end of 4 quarters, the game goes into overtime. Overtime is different depending on the level of play. For NFL games, the game goes into "sudden death." A coin toss determines which team receives the ball, and the first team to score wins the game. If neither team scores at the end of 15 minutes, the game is declared a tie. High school and college overtime periods give each team an equal opportunity to try and score. Both teams get possession of the ball on their opponent's 25-yard line to score either a touchdown or a field goal. Their possession ends if they score, lose the ball on a fumble or interception, or fail to get a first down. Then the defense takes possession of the ball on their opponent's 25-yard line. If the teams are still tied going into the 3rd overtime period, each team must attempt to score 2 extra points after each touchdown by running an offensive play to cross the end zone instead of kicking the ball through the uprights for a single point.

How to Play Football

Substitutions

• Substitutes are only allowed to enter the game on a dead ball, and they must leave the field on their sideline.

Starting Play

• A coin is tossed prior to the opening kick-off to determine which team will kick off first and which goals teams will defend. Play begins with a kick off from the 35-yard line at the start of each half and after a score. After a safety, the ball is kicked off from the 20-yard line.

Kick-Offs

• A kick off is a free kick taken from the kicking team's 30-yard line (40-yard line in high school). It may be taken in one of the following ways:

• Football kicking tee

• It can be kicked off of a tee

• It can be drop kicked

• Another player can hold the ball for a place kick

• During kick off, all players have to be inbounds. The kicking team, except for the kicker and the place kick holder, must be behind the ball. The opponent must be at least 10 yards away.

• The ball must travel at least 10 yards. If the opposing team gains possession of the ball, they may advance the ball up the field by running with it. If the kicking team gets the ball, the ball is dead and it's put in play from where it was recovered.

• If the ball is kicked out of bounds (except for the end zone) before being touched by a member of the receiving team, it's an illegal kick. The receiving team can have the kicking team kick it over again from a spot 5 yards closer to the kicking team's goal or they may opt to take it at the spot it went out of bounds or 30 yards from the point of the kick.

Changing Ends

• Teams change goals at the end of the 1st and 3rd quarters, but the relative position of the ball on the field stays the same. For example, if the offensive team had the ball on the 30-yard line at the end of the 1st quarter, the ball is moved to the 30-yard line on the other end of the field and play resumes.

Playing the Ball

• Players can kick, carry, and throw the ball to move it up the field

• A defender may knock down a pass that's in the air

• If the player with the ball touches the ground with any part of his body except his hands or feet or if he goes out of bounds, he is called "down" and the ball is dead

• The offensive team has 25 seconds to put the ball into play on each down from the time the referee marks the spot of the ball

Scrimmage Downs

• Most of the football game takes place during plays, or downs, that begin at the line of scrimmage. The officials "spot" the ball before each down by placing it at a designated spot on the playing field. A down is the period of time that begins when the center puts the ball into play until the ball becomes dead. When a team has the ball, it has 4 downs to advance the ball 10 yards or score. Each time it moves the ball 10 yards down the field, it's awarded a new set of 4 downs. If it fails to advance 10 yards, the ball is given to the other team at the point it became dead at the end of the 4th down.

Football rules

• The line of scrimmage for each team is an imaginary line passing through the end of the football nearest to them, extending from sideline to sideline. The area between these lines, which is the length of the football, is the "neutral zone." Each team lines up at least 7 players on the line of scrimmage who stand on either side of the ball and are parallel to the goal line. These rest of the team, except the player receiving the snap (usually the quarterback), must be at least 1 yard behind the line of scrimmage.

Football basics

The snap is a backward pass through the legs of the center, who puts the ball into play. The snap must be one quick and continuous motion, and the snapper can't move his feet or lift a hand until after the ball is snapped. Other players have to stay still until the ball is snapped. No one is allowed to enter the neutral zone or move toward his opponent's goal line at a snap. The snap must be to a player behind the line of scrimmage, unless it touches the ground.

Fair Catch

• After the ball has been kicked on a punt or kick-off, the player receiving the kick may signal a fair catch by raising one arm straight up in the air. By giving this signal, he has the right to catch the ball without being tackled by any member of the kicking team. The ball is dead at the spot of the catch. The receiver gives up the right to try and advance the ball up the field when he gives a fair catch signal.

Backward Pass

• A runner can make a backward pass at any time. A teammate may catch the pass or recover it if it hits the ground.

Fumble

• If a player loses the ball and it leaves his hands, play continues no matter which team recovers it and whether or not it touches the ground.

Interception

• An interception is a pass that's caught by a defensive player while it's still in the air. Possession of the ball belongs to the team that intercepted it.

Forward Pass

The offensive team is allowed one forward pass during each play from the line of scrimmage, but the passer must be behind the line of scrimmage when releasing the ball. Any other forward pass is illegal. Any of the defenders are eligible to intercept a forward pass, but the only offensive players that may catch a forward pass are those who are on the ends of the scrimmage line (except the center, guard, or tackle), or are standing at least 1 yard behind the line of scrimmage.

On any forward pass, the ball becomes dead when it:

• goes out of play

• hits the ground

• hits the goalpost

Tackling

• Tackling is when defensive players use their bodies to bring the player with the ball to the ground.

Blocking

Defensive players use their bodies above the knees to block, or impede, the progress of the opponent. The blocker's hands must be closed and kept inside the elbows. The arms may not be extended to push. Blockers are not allowed to hold on to an opponent, and they can't interfere with a pass receiver, a fair catch, a kicker, or a passer. Blocks can't occur below the knees or in the back. The runner with the ball can use his hands and arms to fend off a defender.

Scrimmage Positions

All of the players line themselves up in formation on both sides of the line of scrimmage. There are very specific rules regarding how the players can line up.

7 players called "linemen" must line up directly on the scrimmage line

4 players called "backs" line up behind the line of the scrimmage

Within this formation, there are only 6 players who are allowed to catch a forward pass during a play

Offensive players often line up on the scrimmage line in the following order:

• Left End (tight end, split end, or wide receiver)

• Left Tackle

• Left Guard

• Center

• Right Guard

• Right Tackle

• Right End

These are the offensive positions behind the line of scrimmage:

• Quarterback

• Running Backs (halfback, fullback)

The following positions are on the defensive side of the ball. These players can line up in a variety of ways:

• Linebackers

• Defensive Ends

• Defensive Tackles

• Defensive Backs

Scoring

Touchdown = 6 points.

• It occurs when a player carries the ball into the opponent's end zone or catches a pass while in the end zone.

Football rules

Extra Point = 1 point or 2 points (also known as PAT, point after touchdown).

After a team scores a touchdown, they get the opportunity to earn 1 extra point by kicking the ball through the uprights on the goal post. The ball is placed on the 2-yard line, and both teams line up on the scrimmage line for the kick. The distance of the extra point kick is 20 yards. The scoring team may opt to go for 2 points instead. The ball is still placed at the 2-yard line, but instead of kicking it, they try to get it into the end zone again either by a run or pass. If they're successful in crossing the goal line with the ball, they earn 2 extra points.

Field Goal = 3 points

On a team's 4th down, if they don't feel they will be able to advance the ball far enough for a 1st down and they feel they are within kicking range, they may attempt to kick a field goal from the line of scrimmage. If the ball goes through the goal post, they earn 3 points. If the kick is unsuccessful, the opposing team gets possession of the ball at the line of scrimmage or the 20-yard line (whichever is farther from the goal line).

Safety = 2 points

A safety is called when an offensive player is tackled with the ball in their own end zone. When this happens the defensive team is awarded 2 points, and the team that was scored on has to kick off from their 20-yard line.

Dead Ball

A dead ball marks the end of a down. The ball becomes dead when:

• the ball carrier is downed

• there's an incomplete pass

• the ball or ball carrier goes out of bounds

• a team scores

• a fair catch is signaled

• a member of the kicking team gets control of a punt to down it before the receiving team touches it

• a kicked ball stops moving

• a touchback occurs – when a kick lands in the end zone, it is spotted at the 20-yard line to begin play

Out of Play

• When a ball is kicked out of bounds, it is placed at the point where it crossed the sideline. The only exception is for a free kick.

• When a free kick is kicked out of bounds, it is kicked again after moving the ball back 5 yards from the original spot of the kick.

• If a player with the ball runs out of bounds, the ball is placed at the inbounds lines in the center of the field at the point where he went out of bounds.

• If the ball is passed, kicked, or fumbled out of play behind the goal lines by the opposition, the defending team gets possession of the ball at the 20-yard line between the inbounds lines.

Fouls & Penalties

Players may not:

• hit with their fists

• kick or knee a player

• hit or kick a player below the knee

• tackle a player off the field

• tackle a player after the ball is dead

• grab a player's face mask

• deliberately run into a kicker

• run into a passer after he has released the ball

Penalties

Here are some of the more common penalties included in the American football rules (there are many more):

• Blocking below the waist

• Block in the back – contacting a player without the ball in the back

• Clipping – contacting a player without the ball from behind and below the waist

• Delay of game

• Encroachment – a defensive player crossing the line of scrimmage before the ball is snapped

• Face mask – grabbing the face mask of a player in an attempt to tackle him

• False start – any player that moves after he has gotten set at the line of scrimmage before the ball is snapped

• Horse-collar tackle – grabbing the shoulder pads or jersey from behind and yanking the player to the ground

• Intentional grounding – a forward pass that is intentionally thrown incomplete so the passer avoids being tackled for a loss of yards

• Holding – grabbing or pulling a player without the ball

• Offside – a player is on the wrong side of the line of scrimmage when the ball is snapped

• Pass interference - making physical contact with a receiver to keep him from catching the ball

• Personal foul – any kind of conduct or safety-related rule infraction

• Roughing the kicker – tackling or running into the kicker

• Roughing the passer – tackling or hitting a passer after the pass has already been made

When rule violations are called, the following penalties may be assessed:

• Loss of down

• Loss of yards – 5, 10, or 15 yards

Disqualification

• If you're looking to get a fun pick-up football game going, you will definitely need to modify the basic American football rules to fit the size of your group, your available equipment, and the size of your playing field. A very popular modified game is flag football. A fun way for young kids to learn how to play football is through an NFL flag football league. For those kids ready to put on the pads, there are lots of organized youth football leagues in most cities throughout the U.S

Basic Football Rules for Beginners

Learn how to play football and stop feeling clueless watching from the sidelines.

When you say "football" in many parts of the world, most people think of soccer. So, around the globe, football as we know it is often referred to as "gridiron" or "American football." This summary of the basic American football rules will give you a good overview of the game and prepare you to enjoy watching your kid's game or start a pick-up game of your own!

Football Rules

Object

Gridiron football is played by 2 teams with 11 players on the field at a time who attempt to score points by moving the ball down the field across the goal line or by kicking the ball between the upright goal posts. The team with the most points at the end of regulation time is the winner.

Playing Area

The playing field is a rectangle 100 yards long and a little over 50 yards wide. There is a goal line at each end of the field leading into a 10-yard end zone, and at the back of the end zone there is an upright goal post.

Jersey numbers:

• Quarterbacks, punters, placekickers: #1-19

• Running backs and defensive backs: #20-49

• Centers: #50-59 and #60-79

• Offensive guards and tackles: #60-79

• Wide receivers: #80-89 and #10-19

• Tight ends and H-backs: #80-89 and #40-49

• Defensive linemen: #90-99 and #50-79

Aim

The purpose of American football is to move the ball towards the opposition's end zone and ultimately into their end zone (a touchdown). This is achieved by either running with the ball until tackled, or throwing the ball down field to a team mate.

Downs

Downs are the most fundamental part of NFL play. The offensive team moves the ball forward in sections of at least 10 yards. They have four chances (or downs) to gain those 10 yards. Each time the ball is advanced at least 10 yards within their four chances, another first down is earned, with four more chances to go a further 10 yards. If the offensive team fails to move 10 yards within four downs, possession is surrendered. However, the ball is usually punted to the defending team on fourth down.

Goal posts Teams

• There are 11 players from each team on field at any one time

• Timing

• Four 15min quarters

• Three time-outs per half for each team

• 12min half-time

• 15min sudden-death overtime if scores are tied

Scoring

A touchdown is worth six points, and is scored when a team crosses the opposition's goal line with the ball, or catches or collects the ball in the end zone. A Field goal is worth three points. Field goals are usually attempted on fourth down if the kicker is close enough to the end zone to kick the ball through the posts. An extra point is earned by kicking the ball through the uprights after a touchdown. The team can go for two points by taking the ball into the end zone again. Two points is awarded to the defensive team for a safety when a member of the offensive team is tackled with the ball in his own end zone.

Football Kicking Technique

Score at Least 5 More Points Per Game By Coaching Football Kicking Properly

I'll bet you're frustrated that your team's football kicking skills are leaving at least five points on the field every game you coach. Think about it, how often have you been in a fourth and three situation on the opposition's fifteen yard line with no confidence in hitting the field goal? You go for it instead of trying the kick and don't make it. Instead of a three point lead, your opponent takes over and drives down for a touchdown. If you could improve your team's kicking skills to the point of making just one field goal and two extra points per game, what would those five points do for your football coaching record?

Football Kicking Tips

Let's discuss five simple tips for football kicking to help your kicker eliminate bad technique and have more success.

• Instill in your football kicker the need to invest consistent practice time on developing his kicking skills. This may sound obvious, but too many youth football teams spend so little time working on their kicking game, it's no wonder they can't get the football through the uprights.

• Here's another obvious one, but worth mentioning. Teach your kicker to kick with the side of the foot ("soccer style") as opposed to the "straight on" method. Your kicker will automatically become more accurate using this style of kicking.

• The plant foot is critical. Teach your kicker to place his plant foot alongside the ball, not behind it and not ahead of it. As contact is made with the ball, the bottom of the shoe should be about parallel to the field.

• Pay close attention to the follow-through. Your kicker's head should stay down and remain focused on seeing his foot make contact with the bottom third of the football. Help your kicker avoid a common football kicking mistake by teaching him to keep his head down as long as possible on the follow-through. Make sure the follow-through is aimed straight toward the target.

• Lastly, many young football kickers have a tendency to alter their approach mechanics on longer field goal tries. Help them be aware of this and teach them to keep their approach consistent no matter the length of the attempted kick.

Rosters

We'll discuss NFL rules and procedures soon, but first, it's important to understand the specific players that make up each football roster. Each team starts 11 offensive players and 11 defensive players with a handful of special teams players seeing the field on specific plays (more on that later). The following are the various positions in football:

Offense Positions

• Quarterbacks (QB): receive the football from the center and throw it to pass-catchers, main decision-maker for the offense

• Running Backs (RB): take the ball from the quarterback in the "backfield" and carry it up the field, also known as a Half-Back (HB)

• Fullbacks (FB): less common in the modern NFL but help with blocking for running backs or protecting quarterbacks

• Wide Receivers (WR): downfield pass-catchers, responsible for receiving the ball from the quarterback on passes

• Tight Ends (TE): typically bigger than wide receivers, can serve as pass-catchers or assist the offensive line as blockers in the run/pass game

• Offensive Tackles (OT): each team has a right tackle and a left tackle, they line up on the ends of the offensive line and protect the quarterback against "pass rushers" or block defenders to open up holes for running backs

• Offensive Guards (OG): each team has a right guard and left guard, they line up on the interior of the offensive line inside of each of the tackles and on either side of the center, they serve similar a similar role to tackles

• Center (C): each team starts one center that "snaps" the ball to the quarterback at the beginning of each play and helps with run and pass blocking

Defense Positions

• Defensive Tackles (DT): each team starts one or two defensive tackles depending on whether they are running a 3-4 or 4-3 front; defensive tackles are some of the biggest players on the field and specialize in clogging the middle of the field to defend against running backs, although some are also fast enough to get to the quarterback

• Defensive Ends (DE): these players line up on either side of the defensive tackle(s) and either set the edge of the defense against the running back or work to get around the offensive tackles to put pressure on the opposing quarterback

• Outside Linebackers (OLB): in 3-4 defenses, outside linebackers are crucial as the players who put pressure on the quarterback on the edge of the defense in the "pass rush"

• Inside Linebackers (ILB): 3-4 defenses have two inside linebackers while 4-3 defenses have three linebackers serving a variety of roles; inside linebackers are often the leader of the defense, responsible for calling out adjustments, stopping the run game, and defending the middle of the field

• Cornerbacks (CB): these players will line up against wide receivers in the passing game in either man-to-man coverage (1-on-1 against a receiver) or in a zone formation where they cover a specific part of the field

• Free Safety (FS): free safeties are often the "center fielder"; they prevent big plays from occurring and assist cornerbacks in pass coverage in the deeper third of the field

• Strong Safety (SS): strong safeties have much more versatility in where they line up on the field, contributing to the pass rush, pass coverage, and run defense; they will often line up "in the box" or with the linebackers as an extra defender closer to the line of scrimmage

Defense Formations

There are several nuances to each defensive formation that you see below, but the basic idea is that a 3-4 defense will line up with 3 defensive linemen and 4 linebackers while a 4-3 defense will line up with 4 defensive linemen and 3 linebackers; most teams use a combination of both schemes

3-4 Defense Formation

3-4 defenses feature three defensive linemen (one defensive tackle and two defensive ends) alongside four linebackers (two outside and two inside). To break it down further, linebackers are often referred to the Will (weakside), Sam (strongside), Mike (middle), and Jack. The Jack is not present in 4-3 defenses and replaces what would have been an additional down lineman. The Jack is a defensive end/outside linebacker hybrid (i.e. Von Miller) and rushes the passer or the running back on pretty much every play.

4-3 Defense Formation

In a 4-3 defense, the Jack linebacker is replaced with an additional defensive lineman (in this case a defensive tackle). The Mike linebacker still lines up in the middle and the Will/Sam linebackers will fill a variety of roles. In this formation, the OLB #9 is the Sam linebacker because the opposing team's tight end is lined up on the line of scrimmage on his side. TE #38 is more of a slot receiver in this formation and his off-alignment will allow OLB #47 an easier path to the quarterback – this is the Will.

Kicking Positions

• Kickers (K): typically the most utilized member of the special teams, kickers are responsible for two things: (1) they kick-off at the beginning of each half or after a scoring play, (2) they attempt to kick the ball through the goalposts on field-goal attempts.

• Punters (P): these players are utilized as specialists on fourth-down plays when the offense cannot convert the first down and decides to punt the ball away, more on this later

• Returners (KR/PR): each team has kick and punt returners, sometimes the same player, who receives the ball on kickoffs or punts and attempts to gain extra yardage for the offense

• Long Snappers (LS): on field goal attempts and punts, the special teams will use a long snapper which can snap the ball further than the center usually does

• Gunners: on special teams defense, the gunners are the players who run downfield and attempt to tackle the returner; special teams players are almost always players who fill other positions on the team as well

Kicking Formations

This is the formation you will see either to start the first or second half or immediately following a score by the kicking team (the black team here). Alongside the kicker will be 10 players who are known as the gunners – these players are some of the fastest runners or hardest hitters on the roster and typically won't be heavily relied upon as starters on defense or offense. The receiving team will have two returners back on either side – in this case, WR 12 and 38. One of those returners will catch the football and attempt to run it up field while the rest of his special team's teammates attempt to block the gunners and create space for him. If the offensive team is unable to convert by the fourth down, they will often attempt a field goal (if in range). Here, we see the kicking team lining up from about the 18-yard line to kick a field goal. This is also where the extra point or PAT is attempted from. The kicker (4) is responsible for kicking the ball through the uprights while his teammate, the punter (3), holds the ball for him. This can also commonly be the backup quarterback on the roster. The rest of the players on the field for the kicking team are responsible for blocking the opposing players while they attempt to get around or over the line of scrimmage to block the kick. If they successfully block the kick, they have an opportunity to run downfield with the football if they can catch it before it touches the ground.

Punting Formation punting

Punt coverage is very different from kickoff coverage, as you can see from this picture. The players are much more crowded at the line of scrimmage as this takes place as a normal offensive snap would – with players within a few feet of each other at the time of the snap. It's rare for any players other than the punt returner to be set up downfield as the returning team will attempt to crowd the line of scrimmage to try to block the punt. The punting team will leave several players on the line of scrimmage to protect the punter and give him time to boot the ball downfield.

Rules

Gaining a full understanding of the rules of football is likely the biggest obstacle to learning the game as a beginner. The NFL has a complex and long rulebook – in fact, there's a 92-page PDF you can download from their official site. I'm going to break it down to the basics here:

• Field Dimensions: NFL games are played on fields that are 100 yards in length and 53 yards in width. Each set of "downs" occurs over a 10-yard chunk of space. The end zone is a 10-yard set of space on either end of the field – if the offense reaches this spot, it counts as a touchdown. In the back of the end zone are goalposts – each is 10 feet high and 18 feet, 6 inches wide.

• Timing: NFL games are played over the duration of 60 minutes, which are split into four quarters. At the beginning of the two halves, a kickoff will occur. To determine which team receives this kickoff, a coin toss will occur at the beginning of every game. The winner of this coin toss can determine whether it would prefer to receive the opening kickoff or "defer" to the second half – there are strategic benefits to either option. If the game is tied in score after the four quarters an overtime period will occur.

• Timeouts/Play Clock: Each team gets three timeouts in each half which they can use at any point during the half. Unused timeouts from the first half do not carry over to the second half. Each half also has a 2-minute warning with 2 minutes remaining in the half in which the clock is automatically stopped. There is also a play clock on every down which lasts 40 seconds timed from the end of the previous down. The game clock is automatically stopped if there is an incompletion or a player runs out of bounds, but the play clock is always running.

• First Downs: Each time the offense has the ball, they have four tries or "downs" to gain 10 yards. If it successfully gains 10 yards, it earns a "first down" and another set of four downs. If the offense reaches fourth down, it will usually punt (kick) the ball away to force the opposing team to begin their drive from worse field position. If an offense attempts to convert on fourth down and fails, a turnover on downs occurs where the opposing team takes over at that exact spot on the field.

• Kickoff: At the beginning of every half of play, or immediately following scored points, one team will kick off to the other team from the defense's 35-yard line to switch possession – this is one of the biggest parts of a kicker's job. On the opposing team, a kick returner will attempt to catch the ball and run it back up the field. Where he is tackled is where his team will begin their offensive drive. If the returner takes a knee, his team will start from the spot where his knee touched the field. If the ball is kicked through the end zone, the returner's team will start from the 25-yard line (formerly the 20-yard line). If the ball is kicked into the end zone, the returner can take a knee and accept the ball at the 25-yard line or run out of the end zone and attempt to pick up additional yardage. If the kicking team kicks the ball out of bounds then the opposing team automatically gets the ball at the 40-yard line, so it's important for them to not do that.

• Turnovers: A turnover will occur when a defender takes possession of the football away from the opposing team. This can either take place on a fumble or interception. A fumble occurs when the offensive ball carrier loses possession of the football before being tackled to the ground. An interception occurs when a defensive player catches a thrown football that the quarterback intended to be passed to an offensive teammate. After a turnover, the defensive team becomes the offense and the player with possession of the football can attempt to reach the end zone for 6 points. The opposing offense will take over possession wherever their defensive player is tackled.

• Overtime: When the two competing NFL teams are tied at the end of regulation time (60 minutes, 4 quarters) they will play a 10-minute overtime period. Before overtime, a coin toss will occur which determines which team receives the ball to start overtime. Each team must possess or have the opportunity to possess the football unless the team with possession first scores a touchdown on their drive. If the team with possession first scores a field goal, the other team will have the opportunity to match their 3 points (or win with a touchdown). If the team with possession first does not score a touchdown, sudden death scoring comes into play where the next team to score wins the game. Each team gets two timeouts during overtime. If the score of the game is still tied after overtime, the game will end in a tie.

Penalties

The NFL has a system that allows it to discipline team's in-game for not following particular rules – penalties. The penalty structure has seen a lot of criticism in recent years for inconsistent calls by referees. These are the most common penalties which will occur during any given game:

• Holding: This is easily the most common penalty in football and a constant source of frustration for football fans as it is very subjective. Holding can occur on both offensive and defensive players.

• Offensive Holding: When an offensive player grabs/tackles/holds a defensive player in such a way that prevents them from tackling the ball carrier. Penalty – 10 yards.

• Defensive Holding: When a defensive player grabs/tackles/holds an offensive player other than the ball carrier. Penalty – 5 yards, automatic first down.

• False Start: This occurs when an offensive player makes a quick, abrupt movement before the snap of the ball. This can often cause an opposing defensive player to jump offsides which is why it needs to be penalized. The penalty for a false start is 5 yards.

• Encroachment: This is when a defensive player encroaches the line of scrimmage before the ball is snapped, making contact with an opponent. The penalty for encroachment is 5 yards.

• Offsides: This occurs if, when the ball is snapped, any part of a player's body is beyond the line of scrimmage. The penalty for holding is 5 yards. Also known as neutral zone infraction.

• Pass Interference: When the quarterback has attempted a pass and the ball is still in the air if there is illegal contact between the offensive/defensive players it is pass interference.

• Offensive Pass Interference: When an offensive player pushes away a defensive player before making a play on the ball, restricting his ability to defend the pass. Penalty – 10 yards, replay down.

• Defensive Pass Interference: When a defensive player pushes away an offensive player before making a play on the ball, restricting his ability to make the catch. Penalty – the spot of the foul, automatic first down.

• Unnecessary Roughness: This is a personal foul that is designed to protect players who are in a defenseless position from being hit. This is often called for helmet-to-helmet contact. Penalty – 15 yards, automatic first down.

• Horse Collar Tackle: When a defender tackles an offensive player by grabbing inside their shoulder pads or jersey from behind and pulling them down. Penalty – 15 yards, automatic first down.

• Face Mask: When a player grabs inside the face mask of another player when attempting to block or tackle. Penalty – 15 yards, automatic first down.

• Roughing the Kicker/Punter: When a defensive player makes contact with the kicker/punter (unless the defensive player has touched the ball before contact). Penalty – 15 yards, automatic first down.

• Delay of Game: If the offense/defense performs an action which causes the play clock to extend past the 40-second play clock. Penalty – 5 yards.

• Intentional Grounding: When a quarterback is under pressure from the defense and in danger of giving up a sack, they may choose to throw the ball away. If they throw the ball in an area where there is not a receiver in the immediate vicinity, it is intentional grounding. Penalty – 10 yards, loss of down.

Glossary

The following is some of the most typical jargon you will hear associated with the NFL:

Backfield: The area behind the line of scrimmage where the quarterback, fullback, and running back line up.

Down: On each NFL drive, the offense will have four opportunities to earn a first down. These opportunities are known as downs and will be labeled first down, second down, third down, and fourth down.

• Drive: A series of plays for an NFL offense is known as a drive. Drives will end in either a touchdown, field goal, safety, turnover, turnover on downs, or punt.

• End Zone: The 10-yard strip at the end of either side of the 100-yard field is known as the end zone. This is where the offense is attempting to go with the football, if you get inside the end zone you score a touchdown.

• Extra Point: After the offense scores a touchdown, they have an opportunity to tack on an extra point by kicking the ball through the goalpost from 33 yards away.

• Fair Catch: If a kick/punt returner waves his hand in the air on a kick/punt, he is signaling for a fair catch. This means that his offense will start their drive wherever he catches the ball and the opposing players are not permitted to make contact with him.

• Field Goal: If an offense is not able to score a touchdown and gets stuck on fourth down, they may try a field goal attempt which is a kick through the uprights from their current position. Field goal position for most teams starts at around the opposing team's 35-yard line (35 yards + 10 yards in end zone = 45-yard attempt).

• First Down: On an offensive series, the offense will usually need to pick up a series of first downs to move the ball downfield (unless they get one big touchdown at the beginning of the drive). The first down marker is set up 10 yards away from the spot of the ball when the series began or when the last first down was acquired.

• Free Kick: After a team gives up a safety, they will also have to kick the ball to the other team from their 20-yard line on what is known as a dropkick (the kicker starts with the ball in his hands).

• Fumble: If an offensive player with possession of the ball drops it or has it knocked out of his hands, the offense will risk losing possession on the fumble.

• Handoff: This occurs when the quarterback hands the football to the running back behind the line of scrimmage. Running plays can also occur on swing passes and tosses.

• Hash Marks: These are the white markers in the grass that help the players, officials, and fans have a better idea of where the football is in relation to the entire field.

• Huddle: When the offense comes together to discuss strategy prior to the snap of the football, they are going into a huddle. Many teams will run no-huddle offense for stretches to keep defenders tired and on their toes.

• Incompletion: When a quarterback attempts to throw the football to his receiver and the pass is not completed, it is known as an incompletion.

• Interception: This occurs when a defender is able to catch or "pick off" the quarterback's attempted pass and gain possession for his team's offense.

• Kickoff: This occurs when a team kicks the ball off either at the beginning of the first or second half or immediately following a score by the kicking team.

• Line of Scrimmage: The imaginary line where the football is spotted and the offensive line lines up against the defensive line is known as the line of scrimmage.

• Muffed Punt/Kick: When the punt/kick returner is unable to complete the catch of the football on the punt/kick, it is not an incompletion – rather, it practically acts as a fumble. The ball is live and possession can be regained by the kicking team.

• Punt: If an offense is unable to gain a first down on their first three downs and is not in field goal range, they have two options – attempt the conversion on fourth down and risk a turnover on downs or punt the ball away and force the other team to start with worse field position. Teams never seek out to punt the ball on an offensive drive, but that doesn't make it a bad play.

• Red Zone: The area of the field 20 yards away from the defense's end zone is known as the red zone. As the offense gets closer to scoring range, the field shrinks and the defense compresses. This makes red zone play-calling more restricted and offenses rely on strength/power more often.

• Return: After a kick/punt, the player who catches the ball from mid-air and attempts to gain yardage is known as the returner. The yardage he is able to pick up is known as the return.

• Sack: This occurs when the quarterback is "tackled" behind the line of scrimmage, usually resulting in a major loss of yardage for the offense. This is the ultimate goal for every pass rusher in football.

• Safety: When an offensive ball carrier is tackled in their own end zone, this results in two points for the defensive team as well as possession of the ball for their offense.

• Secondary: The group of defenders who line up deeper in the field and typically line up against pass-catchers is known as the secondary – cornerbacks and safeties.

• Snap: Each offensive play is known as a snap as it starts with the snap of the football from the center to the quarterback.

• Special Teams: This is the third facet of the game beyond offense and defense which refers to anything involving kicking, punting, etc.

• Touchdown: If a player is able to get the ball into the opposing end zone, they earn six points for their team – a touchdown.

• Turnover on Downs: If the offensive team is unable to gain a first down on any of their four downs, the drive results in a turnover on downs – the defensive team regains possession of the football at the spot on the field where that fourth-down play ended.

The Complete Beginners Guide To American Football

American football is a team sport played on a rectangular grass or turf surface called a football field. There are a total of 22 players on the field at all times. These players make contact with each other to tackle the player with football. American football is much more than physical contact and big hits among the organized chaos. As one of the more complicated sports globally, American football has many rules, positions, and equipment that make it unique. In this book, I will break down American football and how the game is played for beginners.

Football Tips for Beginners

Tips to better your game at American football. Who wouldn't love to have a chance to experience the thrill this game can offer? After reading this piece you would get on the ground and get throwing! American football is a difficult game which requires the maximum of your physical abilities, strategic thinking, and teamwork. Here we have collected some tips to help you in becoming a better football player when you are only starting.

1. Nothing Can Make You Perfect but Practice

Football Tips for Beginners the best way to improve your skills is to practice. No matter if you play football, teach kids or write novels. The more time you spend on the football field, the better your performance will be. Remember that you should never miss a practice with your team and don't be lazy to do some extra work before or after the training. It will also show your coach that you are devoted and responsible, committed to your team. In your spare time you can find a partner and practice the basic skills: catching, blocking, passing, covering, form tackling and the rest.

2. Rules Should Be Learned

Before you start playing a game, learn the rules. And it is not only about the basic rules, but also the specific aspects of it, as knowing the rules means being aware of all of them. What should you do with a ball when you pick it up? What can your opponent do? The better you know the rules of the game, the more chances you have to win.

3. Use Proper Football Gear

Football accessories are so important when it comes to playing football. You should consider buying a good- quality football equipment. In case it is hard to choose, think about such giants as Under Armor, Nike, Oakley and other sport gear companies.

4. Get Stronger and Faster

Take your time at the gym. Put your main effort on improving your strength and mass, agility and speed. Remember that your goal is to increase your performance, but not to shape a perfect body, as many beginners do. Good idea is to make a workout plan, as it will give you the ability to measure your success and allow you to be consistent in your work.

5. Think What You Eat

A football player should be a strong person. Having a good diet can help your performance. While training can give you only 20% of muscle growth, the food you eat accounts for 80%. Thus you should think about a particular diet. Protein is essential to muscle growth. You can calculate how much protein intake you need be a simple formula. Moderately active people, as usually beginners are, exercise 5-7 times a week, including weight training 3-4 times per week. To calculate the number of grams of protein to eat every day they should multiply their weight in pounds by 0.6.

6. Don't Compete, Just Play

Enjoy every game. Moreover, enjoy the difficulties and new challenges every game brings you. If you win all the games, it is a good reason to consider playing for a team in a higher division. Only challenges will allow you to learn, grow and become a better player.

7. Sleep Enough

Sleep is a vital part of your health. 90% of healing is done during the sleep. It is important to have an everyday sleeping schedule and especially have enough hours of sleep before the game. Alcohol interrupts your sleep cycle and the production of testosterone, which is beneficial for your muscle growth and energy.

Printed in Great Britain
by Amazon

17813712R00037